FREEDOM
& Truth

A Practical Guide for Acquiring
Spiritual Power and Peace

JAMES ALLEN

Author of *As a Man Thinketh*

Freedom and Truth by James Allen
Public Domain. Reprint edition by Sound Wisdom, 2021

Published and Distributed by
SOUND WISDOM
PO Box 310
Shippensburg, PA 17257-0310
717-530-2122
info@soundwisdom.com
www.soundwisdom.com

ISBN 13: 978-1-64095-331-4
ISBN eBook: 978-1-64095-332-1

Note: This book is a product of its time and does not reflect the same views on race, gender, sexuality, ethnicity, and interpersonal relations as it would if it were written today.

For Worldwide Distribution, Printed in the U.S.A.
1 2 3 4 5 6 / 25 24 23 22 21

CONTENTS

CONTENTS

CHAPTER ONE

THE ACQUISITION OF POWER

The world is full of people who are seeking pleasure, excitement, and novelty rather than strength, stability, and power. In pursuing the former, they are actively diminishing whatever power they have. It is difficult to find men and women of real power and influence, because few are prepared to make the sacrifice necessary to acquire power and even fewer are ready to patiently build up character.

Those who are vulnerable to the whims of their fluctuating thoughts, emotions, and impulses are weak and powerless. Strength and power are found in the ability to control and direct these forces. Although individuals with strong passions may seem fierce, their intensity is not true power. The elements that contribute to power might be present, but ferocity must be tamed and subdued by a higher intelligence in order to access real power. To grow in power, individuals must awaken themselves to consecutively higher states of consciousness and intelligence.

Nor is self-control the distinguishing feature between an individual of weakness and one of power. Stubborn individuals may possess willpower, but they are weak and foolish. Real power lies only in heightened consciousness and intelligence. The pleasure-seekers, the lovers of excitement, the hunters after novelty, and the victims of impulse and hysterical emotion lack the knowledge of principles that provide balance, stability, and influence.

Individuals begin to develop power when they master their impulses and selfish inclinations, steady themselves on the higher and calmer consciousness within them, and anchor their thoughts and actions in concrete, universal principles.

The key to accessing the highest power available to humankind is found in recognizing unchanging principles and embedding them in one's consciousness. When, after much searching, suffering, and sacrificing, the light of an eternal principle dawns upon the soul, a divine calm ensues and joy unspeakable gladdens the heart. An individual who has realized such a principle ceases to wander and remains poised and self-possessed. He or she ceases to be "passion's slave" and becomes a master-builder in the Temple of Destiny.

Individuals who are governed by self rather than a principle change face whenever their selfish comforts are threatened. They adopt whatever means necessary to defend and guard their own interests. They are continually scheming as to how they may protect themselves against their enemies, being too narcissistic to perceive that they are their own enemy. The work of such individuals crumbles away, for it is divorced from Truth and power. All effort that is grounded upon self perishes; the only work that endures is that which is built upon an indestructible principle.

All effort that is grounded upon self perishes; the only work that endures is that which is built upon an indestructible principle.

People who stand upon a principle are the same calm, dauntless, self-possessed individuals under all circumstances. When a trial comes that forces them to choose between their personal comforts and Truth, they give up their comforts and remain firm on their principle. Even the prospect of torture and death cannot alter or deter them. Whereas individuals ruled by self regard the loss of their wealth, their comforts, or their life as the greatest calamities that can befall them, individuals of principle look upon these incidents as insignificant in comparison with the loss of character or Truth. To desert Truth is, to them, the only event that could really be called a calamity.

It is the hour of crisis that determines who are the minions of darkness and who are the children of light. It is impending disaster, ruin, and persecution that separates the sheep from the goats and reveals to the reverential gaze of succeeding generations the men and women of power.

It is easy for individuals who possess all their creature comforts to convince themselves that they believe in and adhere to the principles of Peace, Brotherhood, and Universal Love. But oftentimes when their enjoyments are threatened, or if they imagine them to be threatened, they show that they believe in and stand upon strife, selfishness, and hatred, rather than Peace, Brotherhood, and Love.

In contrast, individuals of power do not desert their principles when threatened with the loss of every earthly thing, including even the loss of reputation and life. The words and contributions of these individuals will endure throughout history; their lives

will be celebrated long after their death. Take the life of Jesus Christ as an example: rather than desert the principle of Divine Love on which he rested and in which all his trust was placed, Jesus endured the utmost extremity of agony and deprivation, and today the world worships at his pierced feet in rapt adoration.

There is no way to acquire spiritual power except by the inward illumination and enlightenment resulting from the realization of spiritual principles, and those principles can be realized only through constant practice and application.

There is no way to acquire spiritual power except by the inward illumination and enlightenment resulting from the realization of spiritual principles.

Take the principle of Divine Love, and quietly and diligently meditate upon it with the goal of arriving at a thorough understanding of it. Use it to scrutinize all your habits, your actions, your communication with others, your every secret thought and desire. As you persevere in this course, Divine Love will become more and more perfectly revealed to you, and your own shortcomings will stand out in more and more vivid contrast, spurring you on to renew your efforts. And once you catch a glimpse of the incomparable majesty of that imperishable principle, you will never again rest in your weakness, your selfishness, your imperfection, but will pursue that Love until you have relinquished every discordant element and have brought yourself into perfect harmony with it. That state of internal harmony is spiritual power.

Take also other spiritual principles, such as Purity and Compassion, and apply them in the same way, and so exacting is Truth that you will not be able to rest until the innermost portion of your soul is free of every stain and your heart has become incapable of any hard, judgmental, and pitiless impulse.

Only in so far as you understand, realize, and rely upon these principles will you acquire spiritual power, and that power will be manifested in and through you in the form of increasing objectivity, patience, and self-possession.

The hallmark of divine knowledge is sublime patience. Individuals of power are distinguished by their ability to remain serene amid all the duties and distractions of life. As Ralph Waldo Emerson said, "It is easy in the world to live after the world's opinion; it is easy in solitude to live after our own;

but the great man is he who in the midst of the crowd keeps with perfect sweetness the independence of solitude."

Some mystics hold that perfection in dispassion is the source of that power by which miracles (so called) are performed. Truly those individuals who have gained such perfect control over all their interior forces that no shock, however great, can even momentarily unbalance them must be capable of guiding and directing those forces with a master-hand.

To grow in self-control, in patience, in serenity is to grow in strength and power, and you can only grow in this way by focusing your consciousness upon a principle. To enter the way of power you must, like a child who learns to walk unaided only by a series of attempts and falls, break away from false supports and attempt to stand alone. Free yourself from the tyranny of custom, tradition, conventionality, and the opinions of others until you succeed in walking solitary and upright among your fellow human beings.

> *To grow in self-control,*
> *in patience, in serenity is to*
> *grow in strength and power.*

Rely upon your own judgment; be true to your own conscience; follow the Light that is within you. All outward lights are nothing more than will-o'-the-wisps that will lead you astray. There will be those who will tell you that you are foolish, that your judgment is faulty, that your conscience is all awry, and that the Light within you is darkness—but pay no attention to them. If there is truth to their negative comments, you will discover it on your own in your search for wisdom. Therefore, pursue your course bravely. Your conscience is at least your own, and to follow it is to be a leader; to follow the conscience of another is to be a slave. You will have many falls, suffer many wounds, endure many setbacks for a time, but press on in faith, believing that sure and certain victory lies ahead. Search for a rock, a solid principle, and cling to it once you find it. Get it under your feet and stand firmly upon it until you can succeed in defying the fury of the waves and storms of selfishness.

Rely upon your own judgment;
be true to your own conscience;
follow the Light that is within you.

For selfishness in any and every form is dissipation, weakness, death; unselfishness in its spiritual aspect—in the sense of foregoing of self in the search for higher Truth and consciousness—is conservation, power, life. As you grow in spiritual life and become established upon principles, you will become as beautiful and as unchangeable as those principles, will enjoy the immense satisfaction of their immortal essence, and will recognize the eternal and indestructible nature of the God within.

CHAPTER TWO

THE POWER OF MEDITATION

Spiritual meditation is the pathway to Divinity. It is the mystic ladder that reaches from earth to heaven, from error to Truth, from pain to peace. All saints have climbed it; all sinners must sooner or later come to it, and all weary pilgrims who turn their back upon self and the world and set their face resolutely toward heaven must plant their feet upon its golden rungs. Without its aid you cannot grow into the divine state, the divine likeness, the divine peace, and the unfading glories and pure joys of Truth will remain hidden from you.

Meditation is the intense dwelling, in thought, upon an idea or theme, with the object of thoroughly comprehending it until you become like it and, eventually, one with it. Whatever you constantly meditate upon you will not only come to understand, but will grow more into its likeness, for it will become incorporated into your very being and will become, in fact, your very self. If, therefore, you constantly focus on selfish and debasing thoughts, you will ultimately become selfish and debased. If you continuously think about that which is pure and unselfish, you will surely become pure and unselfish.

> *Meditation is the intense dwelling, in thought, upon an idea or theme, with the object of thoroughly comprehending it until you become like it and, eventually, one with it.*

Tell me what you think about most frequently and intensely, what your soul most naturally turns to in your silent hours, and I will tell you what place of pain or peace you are traveling and whether you are growing into the likeness of the divine or the depraved.

There is an unavoidable tendency to become literally the embodiment of that quality upon which one most constantly thinks. Therefore, let the object of your meditation be above and not below, so that every time you revert to it in thought you will be lifted up. Let it be pure and unmixed with any selfish element so that your heart will become purified and drawn nearer to Truth and not defiled and dragged more hopelessly into error.

Meditation, in the spiritual sense in which I am now using it, is the secret of all growth in spiritual life and knowledge. Every prophet, sage, and savior became such by the power of meditation. Buddha meditated upon the truth until he could say, "I am the Truth." Jesus brooded upon the Divine imminence until at last he could declare, "I and my Father are One."

Meditation centered upon divine realities is the very essence and soul of prayer. It is the silent reaching of the soul toward the Eternal. Mere petitionary prayer without meditation is a body without a soul and is powerless to lift the mind and heart above sin and affliction. If you are praying for wisdom, peace, loftier purity, and a fuller realization of Truth every day, and yet the object of your prayers is still far from you, it means that you are praying for one thing while living out another in thought and action. If you will take your mind off those worldly things that you selfishly cling to, if you will no longer ask God to grant you that which you do not deserve or to bestow upon you the love and compassion that you refuse to bestow on others, but will begin to think and act in the spirit of Truth, you will day by day be growing into those divine realities so that ultimately you will become one with them.

Meditation is the silent reaching of the soul toward the Eternal.

Anyone who wants to secure a worldly advantage must be willing to work vigorously for it. It would indeed be foolish to think that such an advantage would come to those who wait with their hands folded, expecting it to come to them simply because they asked for it. Do not then make the mistake of thinking that you can obtain heavenly possessions without putting forth an effort. Only when you begin to work earnestly in the kingdom of Truth will you be allowed to partake of the Bread of Life. And when you have, by patient and uncomplaining effort, earned the spiritual wages you are requesting, they will not be withheld from you.

If you genuinely seek Truth and not merely your own gratification, if you love it above all worldly pleasures and gains— more, even, than happiness itself—you will be willing to make the effort necessary for its achievement.

If you desire to be freed from sin and sorrow, if you would like to enjoy that spotless purity for which you long and pray, if you would obtain wisdom and knowledge and enter into the possession of profound and abiding peace, come now and enter the path of meditation and let the supreme object of your meditation be Truth.

At the outset, meditation must be distinguished from idle reverie. There is nothing dreamy and unpractical about it. It is a process of searching and uncompromising thought that allows nothing to remain but the simple and naked truth. By meditating in this way, you will no longer build yourself up in your prejudices; rather, forgetting self, you will remember only that you are seeking the Truth. And so you will remove, one by one, the errors that you have built around yourself in the past and will patiently wait for the revelation of Truth that will come when your errors have been sufficiently removed. In the silent humility of your heart you will realize that there is a place deep within the core of our being where Truth abides in fullness, enveloped by the weak flesh that predisposes us to err. Rather than looking for some external illumination, we can access the perfect, clear perception of Truth by opening a path for this imprisoned internal splendor to escape.

To be spiritually awakened is also to be mentally and physically awakened. The sluggard and the self-indulgent can have no knowledge of Truth. The person who, possessed of health and strength, wastes the calm, precious hours of the silent morning in drowsy indulgence is totally unfit to climb the heavenly heights.

To be spiritually awakened is also to be mentally and physically awakened.

The person whose consciousness has become awakened to its lofty possibilities—who is beginning to shake off the darkness of ignorance in which the world is wrapped—rises before the sun, grapples with the darkness within his or her soul, and strives, by holy aspiration, to perceive the light of Truth while the sleeping world dreams on.

No saint, no holy person, no teacher of Truth ever lived who did not rise early in the morning. Jesus habitually rose early and climbed the solitary mountains to engage in holy communion. Buddha always rose an hour before sunrise and engaged in meditation, and all his disciples were enjoined to do the same.

If you have to start your daily responsibilities at a very early hour and therefore cannot dedicate time in the morning to systematic meditation, try to give an hour at night. And if the length and taxing nature of your work prevents you from meditating at night, do not despair—for you can turn your thoughts upward in holy meditation while you work, or in the few idle minutes that you currently waste in aimlessness. And should your work be of that kind that becomes automatic through practice, you may meditate while engaged in your duties. Jacob Boehme, that eminent Christian saint and philosopher, realized his vast knowledge of divine things while working long hours as a shoemaker. In every life there is time to think, and the busiest, most laborious is not shut out from aspiration and meditation.

In every life there is time to think.

Spiritual meditation and self-discipline are inseparable. Therefore, you will begin to meditate upon yourself so as to try and understand yourself, for remember, the great object you will have in view will be the complete removal of all your errors so that you can apprehend Truth. You will begin to question your motives, thoughts, and acts, comparing them with your ideal and endeavoring to look upon them with a calm and impartial eye. In this manner, you will continually be gaining more of that mental and spiritual equilibrium without which individuals are helpless straws upon the ocean of life. If you are given to hatred or anger, you will meditate upon gentleness and forgiveness so as to become alive to a sense of your harsh and foolish conduct. You will then begin to dwell in thoughts of love, gentleness, and abounding forgiveness, and as you overcome the lower impulses by the higher ones, there will gradually, silently steal into your heart a knowledge of the Divine Law of Love with an understanding of its bearing upon all the intricacies of life and conduct. And in applying this knowledge to your every thought, word, and act, you will grow more and more gentle, more and more loving, more and more divine. And thus, through the power of meditation, will you overcome every error, every selfish desire, every human weakness. As each sin and each error is thrust out, a fuller and clearer measure of the Light of Truth will illuminate your soul.

By meditating in this way, you will be endlessly fortifying yourself against your own real enemy—your selfish, perishable self—and will be establishing yourself more and more firmly in the divine and imperishable self that is inseparable from Truth. The direct outcome of your meditations will be a calm, spiritual strength that will be your rock and resting place in the struggle of life. Great is the overcoming power of holy thought, and the strength and knowledge gained in the hour of silent meditation will enrich the soul with saving remembrance in the hour of strife, sorrow, or temptation.

As you grow in wisdom by the power of meditation, you will relinquish more and more of your selfish desires, which are fickle, impermanent, and the source of sorrow and pain, and you will take your stand upon unchangeable principles with increasing steadfastness and trust, enabling you to experience heavenly rest.

Meditation is the means to acquire the knowledge of eternal principles, and the power that results from meditation is the ability to rest upon and trust those principles and so become one with the Eternal. The end of meditation is, therefore, direct knowledge of Truth, God, and the realization of divine and profound peace.

Let your meditations initiate from the ethical ground that you now occupy. Remember that you are to *grow* into Truth by steady perseverance. If you are a Christian, meditate ceaselessly upon the spotless purity and divine excellence of the character of Jesus, and apply his every precept to your inner life and outward conduct so as to approximate more and more toward his perfection. Do not be like those religious individuals who, refusing to meditate upon the Law of Truth and to put into practice the principles given to them by their Master, are content to formally worship, to cling to their particular creeds, and to continue in the endless round of sin and suffering. Strive to rise, by the power of meditation, above all selfish clinging to partial gods or party creeds; above dead formalities and lifeless ignorance.

Walking the highway of wisdom with your mind fixed upon the spotless Truth, you will not rest until you have fully realized it. The individual who earnestly meditates first perceives a truth at a distance and then apprehends it by daily practice. It is only the doer of the Word of Truth who can know of the doctrine of Truth, for although the Truth is perceived by pure thought, it is actualized only by practice.

Although the Truth is perceived by pure thought, it is actualized only by practice.

Buddha said, "He who gives himself up to vanity, and does not give himself up to meditation, forgetting the real aim of life and grasping at pleasure, will in time envy him who has exerted himself in meditation," and he instructed his disciples in the following "Five Great Meditations":

"The first meditation is the meditation of love, in which you so adjust your heart that you long for the weal and welfare of all beings, including the happiness of your enemies.

"The second meditation is the meditation of pity, in which you think of all beings in distress, vividly representing in your imagination their sorrows and anxieties so as to arouse a deep compassion for them in your soul.

"The third meditation is the meditation of joy, in which you think of the prosperity of others and rejoice with their rejoicings.

"The fourth meditation is the meditation of impurity, in which you consider the evil consequences of corruption, the effects of sin and diseases. How trivial often the pleasure of the moment, and how fatal its consequences.

"The fifth meditation is the meditation on serenity, in which you rise above love and hate, tyranny and oppression, wealth and want, and regard your own fate with impartial calmness and perfect tranquility."

By engaging in these meditations, the disciples of the Buddha arrived at a knowledge of the Truth. But whether you engage in these particular meditations or not matters little so long as your object is Truth, so long as you hunger and thirst for that righteousness that is a holy heart and a blameless life.

In your meditations, therefore, let your heart grow and expand with ever-broadening love, until, free from all hatred, and passion, and condemnation, it embraces the whole universe with thoughtful tenderness. As the flower opens its petals to receive the morning light, so open your soul more and more to the glorious light of Truth. Soar upward upon the wings of aspiration; be fearless, and believe in the loftiest possibilities. Believe that a life of absolute meekness is possible; believe that a life of stainless purity is possible; believe that a life of perfect holiness is possible; believe that the realization of the highest truth is possible. If you believe this way, you can climb the heavenly hills rapidly, while the unbelievers continue to grope darkly and painfully in the fog-bound valleys.

Be fearless, and believe
in the loftiest possibilities.

So believing, so aspiring, so meditating, you will enjoy divinely sweet and beautiful spiritual experiences and glorious revelations that will enrapture your inward vision. As you realize the divine Love, the divine Justice, the divine Purity, the Perfect Law of Good, or God, great will be your bliss and deep your peace. Old things will pass away, and all things will become new. The veil of the material universe—which, to the eye of error, is dense and impenetrable, but which, to the eye of Truth, is thin and gauzy—will be lifted and the spiritual universe will be revealed. Time will cease, and you will live only in Eternity. Change and mortality will no longer cause you anxiety and sorrow, for you will become established in the unchangeable and will dwell in the very heart of immortality.

CHAPTER THREE

THE TWO MASTERS: SELF AND TRUTH

Upon the battlefield of the human soul two masters are contending for the crown of supremacy, for the kingship and dominion of the heart: the master of self, also called the "Prince of this world," and the master of Truth, also called the Father God. The master self is the rebellious one whose weapons are passion, pride, greed, vanity, self-will—tools of darkness. The master Truth is the meek and lowly one whose weapons are gentleness, patience, purity, sacrifice, humility, love— instruments of Light.

In every soul, the battle is waged, and as a soldier cannot fight on both sides of a war at once, so every heart is enlisted either in the ranks of self or of Truth. There is no half-and-half course. "There is self and there is Truth; where self is, Truth is not, where Truth is, self is not." These words are from Buddha, the teacher of Truth, and Jesus, the manifested Christ, declared that "No man can serve two masters; for either he will hate the one and love the other, or else he will hold to the one and despise the other. Ye cannot serve God and Mammon."

Truth is so simple, so absolutely un-deviating and uncompromising that it admits of no complexity, no turning, no qualification. Self is ingenious, crooked, and governed by subtle and snaky desire; admits of endless turnings and qualifications; and the deluded worshipers of self vainly imagine that they can gratify every worldly desire and at the same time possess the

Truth. But the lovers of Truth worship Truth with the sacrifice of self, and they ceaselessly guard themselves against worldliness and self-seeking.

Do you seek to know and to apprehend Truth? Then you must be prepared to sacrifice, to renounce to the uttermost, for Truth in all its glory can be perceived and known only when the last trace of self has disappeared.

The eternal Christ declared that he who would be His disciple must "deny himself daily." Are you willing to deny yourself, to give up your lusts, your prejudices, your opinions? If so, you may enter the narrow way of Truth and find that peace from which the world is shut out. The absolute denial, the utter extinction, of self is the perfect state of

Truth, and all religions and philosophies are but many aids to this supreme attainment.

Self is the denial of Truth. Truth is the denial of self. As you let self die, you will be reborn in Truth. As you cling to self, Truth will be hidden from you.

> *Self is the denial of Truth.*
> *Truth is the denial of self.*

While you cling to self, your path will be beset with difficulties, and repeated pains, sorrows, and disappointments will be your lot. There are no difficulties in Truth, and coming to Truth, you will be freed from all sorrow and disappointment.

Truth in itself is not hidden and dark. It is always revealed and is perfectly transparent. But the blind and wayward self cannot perceive it. The light of day is not hidden except to the blind, and the Light of Truth is not hidden except to those who are blinded by self.

Truth is the one Reality in the universe, the inward Harmony, the perfect Justice, the eternal Love. Nothing can be added to it nor taken from it. It does not depend upon any individual, but all individuals depend on it. You cannot perceive the beauty of Truth while you are looking out through the eyes of self. If you are vain, you will color everything with your own vanities. If you are lustful, your heart and mind will be so clouded with the smoke and flames of passion that everything will appear distorted through them. If you are proud and opinionated, you will see nothing in the whole universe except the magnitude and importance of your own opinions.

There is one quality that preeminently distinguishes the person of Truth from the person of self, and that is *humility*. To be not only free from vanity, stubbornness, and egotism, but to regard one's own opinions as of no value, that indeed is true humility.

People who are immersed in self regard their own opinions as Truth and the opinions of others as error. But those humble Truth-lovers who have learned to distinguish between opinion and Truth regard all people with the eye of charity and do not seek to defend their opinion against others, but sacrifice those opinions so that they may love more fully, that they may manifest the spirit of Truth, for Truth in its very nature is beyond description and can only be lived. The individual who has most of charity has most of Truth.

> *The individual who has most*
> *of charity has most of Truth.*

Individuals engaged in heated controversies often foolishly imagine that they are defending the Truth, when in reality they are merely defending their own petty interests and perishable opinions. The follower of self takes up arms against others. The follower of Truth takes up arms against himself. Truth, being unchangeable and eternal, is independent of your opinion and of mine. We may enter into it, or we may stay outside; but both our defense and our attack are superfluous and are hurled back upon ourselves.

Individuals who are enslaved by self—who are passionate, proud, and condemnatory—believe their particular creed or religion to be the Truth and all other religions to be error, and they proselytize with passionate zeal. There is but one religion: the religion of Truth. There is but one error: the error of self. Truth is not a formal belief; it is an unselfish, holy, and aspiring heart, and those who have Truth are at peace with all and cherish all with thoughts of love.

> *There is but one religion: the religion of Truth. There is but one error: the error of self.*

If you silently examine your mind, heart, and conduct, you can determine whether you are a child of Truth or a worshiper of self. Do you harbor thoughts of suspicion, hatred, envy, lust, or pride, or do you strenuously fight against these? If the former, you are chained to self regardless of whatever religion you may profess; if the latter, you are a candidate for Truth, even though outwardly you may profess no religion.

Are you passionate, willful, ever seeking to gain your own ends, self-indulgent, and self-centered, or are you gentle, mild, unselfish, free of every form of self-indulgence, and ever ready to give up your own? If the former, self is your master; if the latter, Truth is the object of your affection.

Do you strive for riches? Do you passionately fight for your party? Do you lust for power and leadership? Are you given to ostentation and self-praise? Or have you given up the love of riches? Have you relinquished all strife? Are you content to take the lowest place and to be passed by unnoticed? And have you ceased to talk about yourself and to regard yourself with self-complacent pride? If the former, even though you may imagine that you worship God, the god of your heart is self. If the latter, even though you may not worship God formally, you are dwelling with the Most High.

The signs by which the Truth-lover is known are unmistakable. Hear the Holy Krishna declare them, in Sir Edwin Arnold's beautiful rendering of the "Bhagavad Gita":

"Fearlessness, single of soul, the will
Always to strive for wisdom; opened hand
And governed appetites; and piety,
And love of lonely study; humbleness,
Uprightness, heed to injure nought which
    lives,
Truthfulness, slowness unto wrath, a mind
That lightly letteth go what others prize;
And equanimity, and charity
Which spieth no man's faults; and
    tenderness
Towards all that suffer; a contented heart,
Fluttered by no desires; a bearing mild,
Modest and grave, with manhood nobly
    mixed,
With patience, fortitude and purity;
An unrevengeful spirit, never given
To rate itself too high—such be the signs,
O Indian Prince! of him whose feet are set
On that fair path which leads to heavenly
    birth!"

When human beings, lost in the devious ways of error and self, have forgotten the "heavenly birth," the state of holiness and Truth, they set up artificial standards by which to judge one another and make their acceptance of, and adherence to, their own particular theology the metric for Truth. And so people are divided one against another, and there is ceaseless enmity and strife and unending sorrow and suffering.

Reader, do you seek to experience the birth into Truth? There is only one way: *Let self die.* All those lusts, appetites, desires, opinions, limited conceptions, and prejudices to which you have previously clung, let them fall from you. Let them no longer hold you in bondage, and Truth will be yours. Cease to look upon your own religion as superior to all others, and strive humbly to learn the supreme lesson of charity. No longer cling to the idea, which generates so much strife and sorrow, that the Savior whom you worship is the only Savior and that the Savior whom your brother or sister worships with equal sincerity and ardor is an imposter. Instead, seek diligently the path of holiness, and you will realize that every holy person is a savior of mankind.

> *Seek diligently the path of holiness, and you will realize that every holy person is a savior of mankind.*

The giving up of self is not merely the renunciation of outward things. It consists of the renunciation of the inward sin, the inward error. The Truth is not merely found by giving up vain clothing, nor by relinquishing riches, nor by avoiding certain foods, nor by speaking smooth words; it is found by giving up the spirit of vanity, by relinquishing the desire for riches, by resisting the demands of instant gratification, by giving up all hatred, strife, condemnation, and self-seeking and becoming gentle and pure at heart. To give up those things without a transformation of heart is Pharisaism and hypocrisy, whereas the latter includes the former. You may renounce the outward world and isolate yourself in a cave or in the depths of a forest, but you will take all your selfishness with you, and unless you renounce that, your wretchedness will be great and your delusion deep. You may remain just where you are, performing all your duties, and yet renounce the world, the inward enemy. To be in the world and yet not of the world is the highest perfection, the most blessed peace, the greatest victory. The renunciation of self is the way of Truth, therefore,

"Enter the Path; there is no grief like hate,
No pain like passion, no deceit like sense;
Enter the Path; far hath he gone whose foot
Treads down one fond offence."

To be in the world and yet not of the world is the highest perfection, the most blessed peace, the greatest victory.

As you succeed in overcoming self, you will begin to see things in their right relations. People who are swayed by any passions, prejudice, like or dislike adjust everything to that particular bias and see only their own delusions. Those individuals who are absolutely free from all passion, prejudice, preference, and partiality see themselves as they are, see others as they are, see all things in their proper proportions and right relations. Having nothing to attack, nothing to defend, nothing to conceal, and no interests to guard, they are at peace. They have realized the profound simplicity of Truth, for this unbiased, tranquil, blessed state of mind and heart is the state of Truth. Those who attain to it dwell with the angels and sit at the footstool of the Supreme. Knowing the Great Law, knowing the origin of sorrow, knowing the secret of suffering, knowing the way of emancipation in Truth, how can such individuals engage in strife or condemnation, for though they know that the blind, self-seeking world, surrounded with the clouds of its own illusions and enveloped in the darkness of error and self, cannot perceive the steadfast Light of Truth and are utterly incapable of comprehending the profound simplicity of heart that has died, or is dying, to self. Yet they also know that at the end of the world, every prodigal son and daughter will come back to the fold of Truth. As so they dwell in good will toward all, regarding everyone with that tender compassion that a parent bestows upon his or her wayward children.

People cannot understand Truth because they cling to self, because they believe in and love self, because they believe self to be the only reality, whereas it is the one delusion. When you cease to believe in and love self, you will desert it and fly to Truth; then will you find the Eternal Reality.

When individuals are intoxicated with the wines of luxury, pleasure, and vanity, the thirst of life grows and deepens within them, and they delude themselves with dreams of fleshly immortality. But when they come to reap the harvest that they sowed and discover that their crops are primarily pain and sorrow, then, crushed and humiliated, relinquishing self and all the intoxications of self, they come with aching hearts to the one immortality, the immortality that destroys all delusions, the spiritual immortality in Truth.

Human beings pass from evil to good, from self to Truth, through the dark gate of sorrow, for sorrow and self are inseparable. Only in the peace and bliss of Truth is all sorrow vanquished. If you suffer disappointment because your cherished plans have been thwarted or because someone has not met your expectations, it is because you are clinging to self. If you suffer remorse for your conduct, it is because you have given way to self. If you are overwhelmed with chagrin and regret because of the attitude of someone else toward you, it is because you have been cherishing self. If you are wounded on account of what has been done to you or said of you, it is because you are walking in the painful way of self. All suffering is of self. All suffering ends in Truth. When you have entered into and realized Truth, you will no longer suffer disappointment, remorse, and regret, and sorrow will flee from you.

> *Only in the peace and bliss of Truth*
> *is all sorrow vanquished.*

"Self is the only prison that can ever bind
   the soul;
 Truth is the only angel that can bid the
   gates unroll;
 And when he comes to call thee, arise and
   follow fast;
 His way may lie through darkness, but it
   leads to light at last."

The woe of the world is of its own making. Sorrow purifies and deepens the soul, and the extremity of sorrow is the prelude to Truth.

Have you suffered much? Have you sorrowed deeply? Have you pondered seriously upon the problem of life? If so, you are prepared to wage war against self and to become a disciple of Truth.

The intellectuals who do not see the necessity for giving up self frame endless theories about the universe and call them Truth. But if you pursue that direct line of conduct that is the practice of righteousness, you will apprehend the Truth that has no place in theory and that never changes. Cultivate your heart. Water it continually with unselfish love and deep-felt pity and strive to shut out from it all thoughts and feelings that are not in accordance with love. Return good for evil, love for hatred, gentleness for ill treatment, and remain silent when attacked. In so doing, you will transform all your selfish desires into the pure gold of Love and self will disappear in Truth. So will you walk blamelessly among others, clothed with the divine garment of humility.

CHAPTER FOUR

THE REALIZATION OF SELFLESS LOVE

It is said that Michelangelo saw in every rough block of stone a thing of beauty awaiting the master-hand to bring it into reality. Similarly, within each of us there sits the Divine Image awaiting the master-hand of Faith and the chisel of Patience to bring it into manifestation. And that Divine Image is revealed and realized as stainless, selfless Love.

Hidden deep in every human heart, though frequently covered up with a mass of hard and almost impenetrable accretions, is the spirit of Divine Love, whose holy and

spotless essence is undying and eternal.
It is the Truth that exists within every
human being; it is that which belongs to the
Supreme—that which is real and immortal.
All else changes and passes away. To realize
this Love by ceaselessly and diligently
practicing the highest righteousness, to live
in it and become fully conscious in it, is to
enter into immortality here and now, is to
become one with Truth, one with God, one
with the central Heart of all things, and to
know our own divine and eternal nature.

> *To realize Divine Love is to enter
> into immortality here and now.*

To reach this Love, to understand and
experience it, you must work with great
persistence and diligence upon your heart
and mind, renewing your patience and

keeping your faith strong, for there will be much work to do before the Divine Image is revealed in all its glorious beauty.

Those who strive to reach and to accomplish the divine will experience many trials and tribulations, and this is absolutely necessary, for how else could one acquire that sublime patience without which there is no real wisdom, no divinity? Now and then, as they proceed, all their work will seem to be futile, and their efforts appear to be wasted. Now and then a hasty touch will mar their image, and perhaps when they imagine their work to be almost completed they will find what they imagined to be the beautiful form of Divine Love utterly destroyed, and they must begin again with their past bitter experience to guide and help them. But those individuals who have resolutely determined to realize the Highest recognize no such thing as defeat.

All failures are apparent, not real. Every slip, every fall, every return to selfishness is a lesson learned, an experience gained, from which a golden grain of wisdom is extracted, helping the strivers toward the accomplishment of their lofty object. To recognize

"That of our vices we can frame
  A ladder if we will but tread
  Beneath our feet each deed of shame"

is to enter the way that leads unmistakably toward the Divine. Those who recognize this understand their failings as dead selves upon which they can rise, as upon stepping-stones, to higher things.

All failures are apparent, not real.

Once you come to regard your failings, sorrows, and sufferings as so many voices telling you plainly where you are weak and faulty, where you fall below the true and the divine, you will then begin to monitor yourself, and every slip, every pang of pain, will show you where you are set to work and what you have to remove out of your heart in order to bring it nearer to the likeness of the Divine, nearer to the Perfect Love. And as you proceed, day by day detaching yourself more and more from the inward selfishness, the Love that is selfless will gradually become revealed to you. And when you are growing patient and calm, when your petulance, tempers, and irritabilities are passing away from you, and the more powerful lusts and prejudices cease to dominate and enslave you, then you will know that the Divine is awakening within you, that you are drawing near to the eternal Heart, that you are not far from that selfless Love, the possession of which is peace and immortality.

Divine Love is distinguished from human loves in one extremely important way: *it is free from partiality*. Human loves cling to a particular object to the exclusion of all else, and when that object is removed, great and deep is the resultant suffering to the one who loves. Divine Love embraces the whole universe, and without clinging to any part, contains within itself the whole. People come to Divine Love by gradually purifying and broadening their human loves until all the selfish and impure elements are burned out of them, thereby preventing suffering. It is because human loves are narrow and confined and mingled with selfishness that they cause suffering. No suffering can result from that Love that is so absolutely pure that it seeks nothing for itself. Nevertheless, human loves are absolutely necessary as steps toward the Divine, and no soul is prepared to partake of Divine Love until it has become capable of the deepest and most intense human love. It is only by passing through human loves and human sufferings that Divine Love is reached and realized.

It is only by passing through human loves and human sufferings that Divine Love is reached and realized.

All human loves are perishable like the forms to which they cling, but there is a Love that is imperishable and that does not cling to appearances.

All human loves are counterbalanced by human hates, but there is a Love that admits of no opposite or reaction, divine and free from all taint of self, that sheds its fragrance on all alike.

Human loves are reflections of the Divine Love and draw the soul nearer to the reality of that Love that knows neither sorrow nor change.

It is well that the mother, clinging with passionate tenderness to the little helpless form of flesh that lies on her bosom, should be overwhelmed with the dark waters of sorrow when she sees it laid in the cold earth. It is well that her tears should flow and her heart ache, for only thus can she be reminded of the fleeting nature of the joys and objects of sense and be drawn nearer to the eternal and imperishable reality.

It is well that lover, brother, sister, husband, wife should suffer deep anguish and be enveloped in gloom when the visible object of their affections is torn from them, so that they may learn to turn their affections toward the invisible Source of all, where alone lasting satisfaction is to be found.

It is well that the proud, the ambitious, the self-seeking should suffer defeat, humiliation, and misfortune—that they should pass through the scorching fires of affliction—for only thus can the wayward soul be brought to reflect upon the enigma of life, only thus can the heart be softened and purified and prepared to receive the Truth.

When the sting of anguish penetrates the heart of human love, when gloom and loneliness and desertion cloud the soul of friendship and trust, it is then that the heart turns toward the sheltering love of the Eternal and finds rest in its silent peace. And whoever comes to this Love is not turned away comfortless, is not pierced with anguish nor surrounded with gloom, and is never deserted in the dark hour of trial.

The glory of Divine Love can be revealed only in the heart that is chastened by sorrow, and the image of the heavenly state can be perceived and realized only when the lifeless, formless accretions of ignorance and self are chipped away.

Only that Love that seeks no personal gratification or reward, that does not make distinctions, and that leaves behind no heartaches can be called divine.

Human beings, clinging to self and to the comfortless shadows of evil, are in the habit of thinking Divine Love as something belonging to a God who is out of reach, as something outside themselves and that must forever remain external to them. Truly, the Love of God is always beyond the reach of self, but when the heart and mind are emptied of self, then the selfless Love, the supreme Love, the Love that is of God or Good becomes an inward and abiding reality.

And this inward realization of holy Love is none other than the Love of Christ that is so much talked about and so little comprehended—the Love that not only saves the soul from sin but lifts it also above the power of temptation.

But how may one attain to this sublime realization? The answer that Truth has always given and will ever give to this question is: "Empty yourself, and I will fill you." Divine Love cannot be known until self is dead, for self is the denial of Love, and how can that which is known be also denied? Not until the stone of self is rolled away from the tomb of the soul does the immortal Christ, the pure Spirit of Love, previously crucified, dead, and buried, cast off the bonds of ignorance and come forth in all the majesty of his resurrection.

You believe that the Christ of Nazareth was put to death and rose again. I am not saying you are wrong in that belief, but if you refuse to believe that the gentle spirit of Love is crucified daily upon the dark cross of your selfish desires, then, I say, you err in this unbelief and have not yet perceived, even from a distance, the Love of Christ.

You say that you have tasted of salvation in the Love of Christ. Are you saved from your temper, your irritability, your vanity, your personal dislikes, your judgment and condemnation of others? If not, from what are you saved, and wherein have you realized the transforming Love of Christ?

The person who has realized the Love that is divine has become a new being and has ceased to be swayed and dominated by the old elements of self. Such an individual is characterized by patience, purity, self-control, deep charity of heart, and unalterable sweetness.

Divine or selfless Love is not a mere sentiment or emotion; it is a state of knowledge that destroys the dominion of evil and the belief in evil and lifts the soul into the joyful realization of the supreme Good. To the divinely wise, knowledge and Love are one and inseparable.

> *To the divinely wise, knowledge and Love are one and inseparable.*

The whole world is moving toward the complete realization of this Divine Love. It was for this purpose that the universe came into existence. Every grasping at happiness— every reaching out of the soul toward objects, ideas, and ideals—is an effort to realize it. But the world does not realize this Love at present because it is grasping at the fleeting shadow and ignoring, in its blindness, the substance. And so, suffering and sorrow continue and must continue until the world, taught by its self-inflicted pains, discovers the Love that is selfless, the wisdom that is calm and full of peace.

All who are willing and ready to give up self and who are prepared to humbly enter into an understanding of everything that the giving up of self involves may attain to and experience this Love, this Wisdom, this Peace, this tranquil state of mind and heart. There is no arbitrary power in the universe, and the strongest chains of fate by which individuals are bound are self-forged. People are chained to that which causes suffering because they desire to be so, because they love their chains, because they think their little, dark prison of self is sweet and beautiful, and they are afraid that if they desert that prison they will lose all that is real and worth having.

The strongest chains of fate by which individuals are bound are self-forged.

The power that dwells within you—which forged the chains and built around itself the dark and narrow prison—can break away when it desires and wills to do so. And the soul does will to do so when it has discovered the worthlessness of its prison, when extended suffering has prepared it for the reception of the boundless Light and Love.

As the shadow follows the form and as smoke comes after the fire, so effect follows cause and suffering and bliss follow the thoughts and deeds of human beings. There is no effect in the world around us that does not have its hidden or revealed cause, and that cause is in accordance with absolute justice. Individuals reap a harvest of suffering because in the near or distant past they have sown seeds of evil; they reap a harvest of bliss also as a result of their own sowing of the seeds of good. Let people meditate upon this, let them strive to understand it, and they will then begin to sow only seeds of good, and they will burn up the tares and weeds that they have formerly grown in the garden of their heart.

The world does not understand the Love that is selfless because it is engrossed in the pursuit of its own pleasures and cramped within the narrow limits of perishable interests, mistaking, in its ignorance, those pleasures and interests for real and abiding things. Caught in the flames of fleshly lusts and burning with anguish, it does not see the pure and peaceful beauty of Truth. Feeding upon error and self-delusion, it is shut out from the mansion of all-seeing Love.

Not having this Love, not understanding it, human beings institute innumerable reforms that involve no inward sacrifice, and they all imagine that their reform is going to right the world forever, while they themselves continue to propagate evil by engaging in it in their own heart. The only thing that can be called reform is that which reforms the human heart, for all evil has its rise there. Not until the world ceases from selfishness and party strife and has learned the lesson of Divine Love will it experience the Golden Age of universal blessedness.

Let the rich stop despising the poor and the poor stop condemning the rich. Let the greedy learn how to give and the lustful learn how to grow pure. Let the partisan cease from strife and the uncharitable begin to forgive. Let the envious endeavor to rejoice with others and the slanderers grow ashamed of their conduct. Let men and women take this course and the Golden Age will be at hand.

Therefore, the person who purifies his or her own heart is the world's greatest benefactor.

The person who purifies his or her own heart is the world's greatest benefactor.

However, the world is, and will be for many ages to come, shut out from that Age of Gold, which is the realization of selfless Love. But if you are willing, you may enter it now by rising above your selfish self, if you will pass from prejudice, hatred, and condemnation to gentle and forgiving love.

Where hatred, dislike, and condemnation are, selfless Love does not live. It resides only in the heart that has discontinued all condemnation.

You say, "How can I love the drunkard, the hypocrite, the sneak, the murderer? I am compelled to dislike and condemn such individuals." It is true that you cannot love such people emotionally, but when you say that you must of necessity dislike and condemn them, you show that you are not acquainted with the Great overruling Love, for it is possible to attain to such a state of internal enlightenment as will enable you to perceive the train of causes by which these individuals have become as they are, to enter into their intense sufferings, and to know the certainty of their ultimate purification. When you possess such knowledge, it will be impossible for you to condemn or dislike them any longer, and you will always think of them with perfect calmness and deep compassion.

If you love people and speak of them with praise until they in some way thwart you or do something you disapprove of, and then you dislike them and speak of them with condemnation, you are not governed by the Love that is of God. If, in your heart, you are continually judging and condemning others, selfless Love is hidden from you.

If, in your heart, you are continually judging and condemning others, selfless Love is hidden from you.

Those individuals who know that Love is at the heart of all things and have realized the incredible power of that Love have no room in their heart for condemnation.

Not knowing this love, people establish themselves as judge and executioner of their fellow human beings, forgetting that there is the Eternal Judge and Executioner. When others hold different views from them and practice different methods for reform, they brand them as fanatical, unbalanced, and lacking judgment, sincerity, and honesty; and when others adhere to their own personal standard, they look upon them as being everything that is admirable—these are the people who are centered in self. But those whose hearts are centered in the supreme Love do not brand and classify their fellow human beings, do not seek to convert others to their own views or convince them of the superiority of their methods. Knowing the Law of Love, they live it and maintain the same calm attitude of mind and sweetness of heart toward all. The debased and the virtuous, the foolish and the wise, the learned and the unlearned, the selfish and the unselfish are all equal recipients of the blessing of their tranquil thought.

You can attain to this supreme knowledge, this Divine Love, only by endlessly practicing self-discipline and by gaining victory over yourself. Only the pure in heart see God, and when your heart is sufficiently purified you will enter into the New Birth, and the Love that does not die, nor change, nor end in pain or sorrow will be awakened within you and you will be at peace.

Those who strive for the attainment of Divine Love are forever seeking to overcome the spirit of condemnation, for where there is pure spiritual knowledge condemnation cannot exist, and only in the heart that has become incapable of condemnation is Love perfected and fully realized.

"He that hateth his brother is a murderer," a crucifier of the divine Spirit of Love, and

until you can regard people of all religions
and of no religion with the same impartial
spirit, with all freedom from dislike, you
have not yet accessed that Love that bestows
upon its possessor freedom and salvation.

The realization of divine knowledge,
selfless Love, completely destroys the spirit
of condemnation, disperses all evil, and
lifts the consciousness to the height of
pure vision, where Love, Goodness, and
Justice are seen to be universal, supreme, all-
conquering, indestructible.

Train your mind in strong, impartial, and
gentle thought. Train your heart in purity
and compassion. Train your tongue to silence
and to true and stainless speech. By so doing,
you will enter the way of holiness and peace

and will ultimately realize the immortal Love. As you live without seeking to convert, you will convince; without arguing, you will teach; not cherishing ambition, the wise will discover you; and without striving to change others' opinions, you will subdue their hearts. For Love is all-conquering, all-powerful, and the thoughts, deeds, and words of Love can never perish.

Train your mind in strong, impartial, and gentle thought. Train your heart in purity and compassion. Train your tongue to silence and to true and stainless speech.

To know that Love is universal, supreme, all-sufficing; to be freed from the constraints of evil; to calm the inward unrest; to know that all individuals are striving to realize the Truth each in their own way; to be satisfied, sorrowless, serene—this is peace; this is gladness; this is immortality; this is Divinity; this is the realization of selfless Love.

CHAPTER FIVE

ENTERING INTO THE INFINITE

From the beginning of time, human beings, in spite of their preoccupation with self, have been intuitively conscious of the limited, fleeting, and illusionary nature of their material existence. In their sane and silent moments, they have tried to cultivate a comprehension of the Infinite and have turned with tearful aspiration toward the restful Reality of the Eternal Heart.

While vainly imagining that the pleasures of earth are real and satisfying, pain and sorrow continually remind individuals of their unreal and unsatisfying nature. Always striving to believe that complete satisfaction is to be found in material things, they are conscious of an inward and persistent revolt against this belief—an internal revolt that is at once a refutation of their essential mortality and an inherent and imperishable proof that only in the immortal, the eternal, the infinite can they find abiding satisfaction and unbroken peace.

And here is the common ground of faith; here is the source of all religion; here is the soul of Fellowship and the heart of Love—that human beings are essentially and spiritually divine and eternal, and that, immersed in mortality and troubled with unrest, they are always striving to become conscious of their real nature.

The spirit of human beings is inseparable from the Infinite and can be satisfied with nothing short of the Infinite. The burden of pain will continue to weigh upon their heart, and the shadows of sorrow to darken their pathway, until, ceasing from their wanderings in the dream-world of matter, they come back to their home in the reality of the Eternal.

> *The spirit of human beings is inseparable from the Infinite and can be satisfied with nothing short of the Infinite.*

As the smallest drop of water detached from the ocean contains all the qualities of the ocean, so do humans, detached in consciousness from the Infinite, contain within them its likeness. And as the drop of water must, by the law of its nature, ultimately find its way back to the ocean and lose itself in its silent depths, so must human beings, by the unfailing law of their nature, at last return to their source and lose themselves in the great ocean of the Infinite.

To re-become one with the Infinite is the goal of human beings. To enter into perfect harmony with the Eternal Law of Wisdom, Love, and Peace. But this divine state is, and must always be, incomprehensible to the merely personal. Personality, separateness, selfishness are one and the same, and they are the antithesis of wisdom and divinity. By the unqualified surrender of the personality, separateness and selfishness cease and individuals enter into the possession of their divine heritage of immortality and infinity.

> *By the unqualified surrender of the personality, separateness and selfishness cease.*

Such surrender of the personality is regarded by the worldly and selfish mind as the most grievous of all calamities, the most irreparable loss, yet it is the one supreme and incomparable blessing, the only real and lasting gain. When a mind is unenlightened about the inner laws of being and the nature and destiny of its own life, it clings to transient appearances, things that have in them no enduring substantiality, and so clinging, perishes, for the time being, amid the shattered wreckage of its own illusions.

Individuals cling to and gratify the flesh as though it were going to last forever, and although they try to forget the nearness and inevitability of its dissolution, the dread of death and of the loss of all that they cling to clouds their happiest hours, and the chilling shadow of their own selfishness follows them like a remorseless specter.

And with the accumulation of worldly comforts and luxuries, the divinity within human beings is drugged, and they sink deeper and deeper into materiality, into the perishable life of the senses, and where there is enough intellect, theories concerning the immortality of the flesh come to be regarded as infallible truths. When a person's soul is clouded with selfishness in any or every form, he or she loses the power of spiritual discrimination and confuses the temporal with the eternal, the perishable with the permanent, mortality with immortality, and error with Truth. It is thus that the world has come to be filled with theories and speculations having no foundation in human experience. Every body of flesh contains within itself, from the hour of birth, the elements of its own destruction, and by the unalterable law of its own nature it must pass away.

The perishable in the universe can never become permanent; the permanent can never pass away; the mortal can never become immortal; the immortal can never die; the temporal cannot become eternal nor the eternal become temporal; appearance can never become reality, nor reality fade into appearance; error can never become Truth, nor can Truth become error. Human beings cannot immortalize the flesh, but, by overcoming the flesh, by relinquishing all its inclinations, they can enter the region of immortality. "God alone hath immortality," and only by realizing the God state of consciousness do humans enter into immortality.

*The perishable in the universe
can never become permanent; the
permanent can never pass away.*

All nature in its myriad forms of life is changeable, impermanent, unenduring. Only the informing Principle of nature of endures. Nature is many and is marked by separation. The informing Principle is One and is marked by unity. By overcoming the senses and the selfishness within, which is the overcoming of nature, individuals emerge from the hard shell of the personal and illusionary and ascend into the glorious light of the impersonal, the region of universal Truth, out of which all perishable forms come.

Let human beings, therefore, practice self-denial; let them conquer their animal inclinations; let them refuse to be enslaved by luxury and pleasure; let them practice virtue, and grow daily into higher and even higher virtue, until at last they grow into the Divine and enter into both the practice and the comprehension of humility, meekness, forgiveness, compassion, and love, the practice and comprehension of which constitute Divinity.

"Goodwill gives insight," and only those who have so conquered their personality that they have but one attitude of mind—that of goodwill toward all creatures—are possessed of divine insight and are capable of distinguishing the true from the false. The supremely good person is, therefore, the wise person, the divine person, the enlightened seer, the knower of the Eternal. Where you find unbroken gentleness, enduring patience, sublime lowliness, graciousness of speech, self-control, self-forgetfulness, and deep and abounding sympathy, look there for the highest wisdom. Seek the company of such an individual, for he or she has realized the Divine, lives with the Eternal, has become one with the Infinite. Do not believe the people who are impatient, given to anger, boastful, who cling to pleasure and refuse to renounce their selfish gratifications, and who do not practice goodwill and far-reaching compassion, for such people do not have wisdom, all their knowledge is vain, and all their works and words will perish, for they are grounded on that which passes away.

Let people abandon self, let them overcome the world, let them deny the personal—by this pathway only can they enter into the heart of the Infinite.

The world, the body, the personality are mirages upon the desert of time, transitory dreams in the dark night of spiritual slumber, and those who have crossed the desert, those who are spiritually awakened have alone comprehended the Universal Reality, where all appearances are dispersed and dreaming and delusion are destroyed.

Let people abandon self, let them overcome the world, let them deny the personal—by this pathway only can they enter into the heart of the Infinite.

There is one Great Law that exacts unconditional obedience, one unifying principle that is the basis of all diversity, one eternal Truth wherein all the problems of the earth pass away like shadows. To realize this Law, this Truth, is to enter into the Infinite, is to become one with the Eternal.

To center one's life in the Great Law of Love is to enter into rest, harmony, and peace. To refrain from all participation in evil and discord, to cease from all resistance to evil and from the omission of that which is good, and to fall back upon unswerving obedience to the holy calm within is to enter into the inmost heart of things, is to attain to a living, conscious experience of that eternal and infinite principle that must always remain a hidden mystery to the sensory-dependent intellect. Until this principle is realized, the soul is not established in peace, and those who realize this are truly wise— not wise with the wisdom of the learned but with the simplicity of a blameless heart and of a divine personhood.

To enter into a realization of the Infinite and Eternal is to transcend time, the world, and the body, which comprise the kingdom of darkness, and to become established in immortality, Heaven, and the Spirit, which make up the Empire of Light.

Entering into the Infinite is not a mere theory or sentiment. It is a vital experience that is the result of constant practice in inward purification. When the body is no longer believed to be, even remotely, the real person; when all appetites and desires are thoroughly subdued and purified, when the emotions are rested and calm, and when the wandering of the mind stops and perfect poise is secured, then—and not until then—is childlike wisdom and profound peace secured.

People grow weary and gray over the dark problems of life and finally pass away and leave them unsolved because they cannot see their way out of the darkness of the personality, being too much engrossed in its limitations.

Seeking to save their personal life, individuals forfeit the greater impersonal Life in Truth. Clinging to the perishable, they are shut out from a knowledge of the Eternal.

All difficulties are overcome by the surrender of self, and there is no error in the universe that cannot be burned up by the fire of inward sacrifice. All problems, no matter how great, will disappear like a shadow under the searching light of self-denial. Problems exist only in our own self-created illusions, and they vanish away when self is yielded up. Self and error are synonymous. Error is involved in the darkness of unfathomable complexity, but eternal simplicity is the glory of Truth.

All difficulties are overcome
by the surrender of self.

Love of self shuts people out from Truth, and seeking their own personal happiness, they lose the deeper, purer, and more abiding bliss. As Thomas Carlyle says, "There is in man a higher than love of happiness. He can do without happiness, and instead thereof find blessedness. …Love not pleasure, love God. This is the Everlasting Yea, wherein all contradiction is solved; wherein whoso walks and works, it is well with him."

Those who have given up that self, that personality that people love and cling to with fierce tenacity, have left behind all perplexity and entered into a simplicity so profoundly simple as to be looked upon by the world, involved as it is in a network of error, as foolishness. Yet such people have realized the highest wisdom and are at rest in the Infinite. They accomplish things without striving, and all problems melt before them, for they have entered the region of reality and deal not with changing effects but with the unchanging principles of things. They are enlightened with a wisdom that is as superior to the process of reasoning as reason is to animality. Having given up their lusts, errors, opinions, and prejudices, they have begun to possess the knowledge of God. Having overcome the selfish desire for heaven and along with it the ignorant fear of hell, and having relinquished even the love of life itself, they have gained supreme bliss and Life Eternal, the Life that bridges life and death and knows its own immortality. Having yielded up all without reservation, they have gained all, and they rest in peace on the bosom of the Infinite.

Only those who have become so free from self as to be equally content to be annihilated are fit to enter into the Infinite. Only those who, ceasing to trust their perishable self, have learned to completely trust the Great Law, the Supreme Good, are prepared to partake of undying bliss.

For such people there is no more regret, nor disappointment, nor remorse, for where all selfishness has ceased, these sufferings cannot be. And whatever happens to them, they know that it is for their own good, and they are content, being no longer the servant of self, but the servant of the Supreme. They are no longer affected by the changes of earth, and when they hear of wars and rumors of wars, their peace is not disturbed. And where men grow angry and cynical and quarrelsome, they bestow compassion and love. Although appearances may contradict it, they know that the world is progressing, and that

"Through its laughing and its weeping,
Through its living and its keeping,
Through its follies and its labors, weaving
in and out of sight,
To the end from the beginning,
Through all virtue and all sinning,
Reeled from God's great spool of Progress,
runs the golden thread of light."

When a fierce storm is raging, none are angered about it, because they know it will quickly pass away. And when the storms of contention are devastating the world, the wise individual, looking with the eye of Truth of pity, knows that it will pass away and that out of the wreckage of broken hearts that it leaves behind the immortal Temple of Wisdom will be built.

Sublimely patient; infinitely compassionate; deep, silent, and pure, their very presence is a benediction; and when they speak, people ponder their words in their hearts and by them rise to higher levels of attainment. Such are they who have entered into the Infinite, who, by the power of utmost sacrifice, have solved the sacred mystery of life.

CHAPTER SIX

THE LAW OF SERVICE

The spirit of Love that is manifested as a perfect and well-rounded life is the crown of being and the supreme end of knowledge upon this earth.

The measure of an individual's truth is the measure of his or her love, and Truth is far removed from the person whose life is not governed by Love. The intolerant and condemnatory, even though they profess the highest religion, have the smallest measure of Truth, while those who exercise patience and listen calmly and dispassionately to all sides, arriving at and helping others toward thoughtful and unbiased conclusions upon all problems and issues, have Truth in fullest

measure. The final test of wisdom is this—
how does a person live? What spirit does
he or she manifest? How does he or she act
under trial and temptation?

> *The final test of wisdom is this—*
> *how does a person live?*

Many people boast of being in possession
of Truth who are continually swayed by grief,
disappointment, and passion and who sink
under the first little trial that comes along.
Truth is nothing if not unchangeable, and
insofar as people take their stand upon Truth
do they become steadfast in virtue, do they
transcend their passions and emotions and
changeable personality.

Human beings formulate perishable
dogmas and call them Truth. Truth cannot

be formulated; it is ineffable and forever beyond the reach of intellect. It can be experienced only by practice; it can be manifested only as a stainless heart and a perfect life.

Truth is beyond the reach of intellect. It can be experienced only by practice.

Who, then, in the midst of the ceaseless pandemonium of schools and creeds and parties, has the Truth? Those who live it. Those who practice it. Those who, having risen above that pandemonium by overcoming themselves, no longer engage in it but sit apart, quiet, subdued, calm, and self-possessed, freed from all strife, all bias, all condemnation, and bestow upon everyone the glad and unselfish love of the divinity within them.

Those who are patient, calm, gentle, and forgiving under all circumstances manifest the Truth. Truth will never be proven by wordy arguments and learned treatises, for if individuals do not perceive the Truth in infinite patience, undying forgiveness, and all-embracing compassion, no words can ever prove it to them.

It is an easy matter for the passionate to be calm and patient when they are alone or amid calmness. It is equally easy for the uncharitable to be gentle and kind when they are dealt with kindly. But those who retain their patience and calmness under all trials, who remain sublimely meek and gentle under the most trying circumstances, they—and they alone—are possessed of the spotless Truth. And this is so because such lofty virtues belonging to the Divine can be manifested only by those who have attained to the highest wisdom, who have relinquished their passionate and self-seeking nature, who have comprehended the supreme and unchangeable Law and have brought themselves into harmony with it.

Therefore, let individuals stop engaging in vain and passionate arguments about Truth, and let them think and say and do those things that contribute to harmony, peace, love, and goodwill. Let them practice heart-virtue and search humbly and diligently for the Truth that frees the soul from all error and sin, from all that afflicts the human heart, and that darkens, as with unending night, the pathway of the wandering souls of earth.

There is one great all-embracing Law that is the foundation and cause of the universe, the Law of Love. It has been called by many names in various countries and at various times, but behind all its names the same unalterable Law may be discovered by the eye of Truth. Names, religions, personalities pass away, but the Law of Love remains. To develop a knowledge of this Law, to enter into conscious harmony with it, is to become immortal, invincible, indestructible.

It is because of the effort of the soul to apprehend this Law that individuals come again and again to live, to suffer, and to die; and when realized, suffering ceases, personality is dispersed, and the fleshly life and death are destroyed, for consciousness becomes one with the Eternal.

The Law is absolutely impersonal, and its highest manifested expression is that of Service. When the purified heart has realized

Truth it is then called upon to make the last, the greatest, and the holiest sacrifice—the sacrifice of the well-earned enjoyment of Truth. It is by virtue of this sacrifice that the divinely freed soul comes to dwell in human beings, clothed with a body of flesh, content to dwell among the lowliest and the least, and to be esteemed the servant of all humankind. That sublime humility that is manifested by the world's saviors is the seal of Godhead. Those people who have annihilated the personality and have become a living, visible manifestation of the impersonal, eternal, boundless Spirit of Love, are alone singled out as worthy to receive the unstinted worship of posterity. Only those who succeed in humbling themselves with that divine humility that is not only the extinction of self but is also the outpouring upon all the spirit of unselfish love, are exalted above measure and given spiritual dominion in the hearts of humankind.

All the great spiritual teachers have denied themselves personal luxuries, comforts, and rewards; have renounced temporal power; and have lived and taught the limitless and impersonal Truth. Compare their lives and teachings, and you will find the same simplicity, the same self-sacrifice, the same humility, love, and peace both lived and preached by them. They taught the same eternal Principles, the realization of which destroys all evil. Those who have been hailed and worshiped as the saviors of mankind are manifestations of the Great impersonal Law and therefore were free from passion and prejudice. Having no opinions and no special letter of doctrine to preach and defend, they never sought to convert or change one's religious opinion. Living in the highest Goodness, the supreme Perfection, their sole objective was to uplift mankind by manifesting that Goodness in thought, word, and deed. They stand between man the personal and God the impersonal and serve as exemplary types for the salvation of self-enslaved humankind.

People who are wrapped up in self and who cannot comprehend the Goodness that is absolutely impersonal deny divinity to all saviors except their own and thus introduce personal hatred and doctrinal controversy. While defending their own particular views with passion, they look upon each other as being heathens or infidels and so render null and void, as far as their lives are concerned, the unselfish beauty and holy grandeur of the lives and teachings of their own masters. Truth cannot be limited; it can never be the special prerogative of any person, school, or nation, and when personality steps in truth is lost.

Truth cannot be limited;
it can never be the special prerogative
of any person, school, or nation.

The glory of the saints, the sages, and the saviors is this—that they have realized the most profound lowliness, the most sublime unselfishness. Having given up all, even their own personality, all their works are holy and enduring, for they are freed from every taint of self. They give, yet never think of receiving. They work without regretting the past or anticipating the future and never look for a reward.

When farmers have tilled and dressed their land and planted the seed, they know that they have done all that they can possibly do, that now they must trust to the elements and wait patiently for the course of time to bring about the harvest, and that no amount of expectancy on their part will affect the result. Similarly, those who have realized Truth go forth as sowers of the seeds of goodness, purity, love, and peace, without expectancy, and never looking for results, knowing that there is the Great Overruling Law that brings about its own harvest in due time and is both the source of preservation and destruction.

Not understanding the divine simplicity of a profound unselfish heart, individuals look upon their particular savior as the manifestation of a special miracle, as being something entirely apart and distinct from the nature of things, and as being, in his or her ethical excellence, eternally unapproachable by the common person. This attitude of unbelief (for this is what it is) in the divine perfectibility of human beings paralyzes effort and binds the souls of human beings as with strong ropes to sin and suffering. Jesus "grew in wisdom" and was "perfected by suffering." What Jesus was, he became such; what Buddha was, he became such; and every holy person became such by unremitting perseverance in self-sacrifice. Once you recognize this, once you realize that by watchful effort and hopeful perseverance you can rise above your lower nature, great and glorious prospects of attainment will open out before you. Buddha vowed that he would not relax his efforts until he arrived at the state of perfection, and he accomplished his purpose.

What the saints, sages, and saviors have accomplished, you likewise may accomplish if you will only follow their path—the way of self-sacrifice, or self-denying service.

Truth is very simple. It says, "Give up self," "Come unto Me" (away from all that defiles) "and I will give you rest." All the mountains of commentary that have been piled upon it cannot hide it from the heart that is earnestly seeking for righteousness. It does not require learning; it can be known without learning. Disguised under many forms by erring, self-seeking individuals, the beautiful simplicity and clear transparency of Truth remains unaltered and undimmed, and the unselfish heart enters into and partakes of its shining radiance. Truth is not realized by weaving complex theories or building up speculative philosophies, but by weaving the web of inward purity—by building up the Temple of a stainless life.

> *Truth is not realized by weaving complex theories or building up speculative philosophies, but by weaving the web of inward purity.*

Those who enter upon this holy way begin by restraining their passions. This is virtue, and it is the beginning of saintship; and saintship is the beginning of holiness. Individuals who are entirely worldly gratify all their desires and practice no more restraint than the law of the land in which they live demands. The virtuous individuals restrain their passions. The saints attack the enemy of Truth in its stronghold within their own hearts and restrain all selfish and impure thoughts, while the holy individuals are those who are free from passion and all impure thought and those to whom goodness and purity have become as natural as scent and color are to the flower. The holy individuals are divinely wise; they alone know Truth in its fullness and have entered into abiding rest and peace. For them evil has ceased; it has disappeared in the universal light of the All-Good. Holiness is the badge of wisdom. Krishna said to Prince Arjuna—

"Humbleness, truthfulness, and
    harmlessness,
Patience and honor, reverence for the wise,
Purity, constancy, control of self,
Contempt of sense-delights, self-sacrifice,
Perception of the certitude of ill
In birth, death, age, disease, suffering
    and sin;
An ever tranquil heart in fortunes good
And fortunes evil...........
.... Endeavors resolute
To reach perception of the utmost soul,
And grace to understand what gain it were
So to attain—this is true wisdom, Prince!
And what is otherwise is ignorance!"

Whoever fights ceaselessly against their
own selfishness and strives to replace it with
all-embracing love are saints, whether they
live in a cottage or amid riches and influence,
whether they preach or remain obscure.

To the worldling who is beginning to aspire toward higher things, the saint, such as a sweet St. Francis of Assisi or a conquering St. Anthony, is a glorious and inspiring spectacle. To the saint, an equally enrapturing sight is that of the sage, sitting serene and holy, the conqueror of sin and sorrow, no longer tormented by regret and remorse, and whom even temptation can never reach. And yet, even the sage is inspired by a still more glorious vision, that of the savior actively carrying out selfless works and using divinity for the common good by sinking himself or herself in the throbbing, sorrowing, aspiring heart of humankind.

And this only is true service—to forget oneself in love toward all, to lose oneself in working for the whole. Those who think their many good works can save them are vain and foolish, as are those who brag of themselves, their work, and their own importance while chained to error. Their fame might be publicized across all the earth, but all their work will come to dust, and they will be reckoned lower than the least in the Kingdom of Truth.

And this only is true service—
to forget oneself in love toward all.

Only the work that is impersonal can live; the works of self are both powerless and perishable. Where duties, however humble, are done without self-interest and with joyful sacrifice, there is true service and enduring work. Where deeds, however brilliant and apparently successful, are done from love of self, there is ignorance of the Law of Service, and the work perishes.

> *Where duties, however humble,*
> *are done without self-interest*
> *and with joyful sacrifice, there is*
> *true service and enduring work.*

It is given to the world to learn one great and divine lesson, the lesson of absolute unselfishness. The saints, sages, and saviors of all time are they who have submitted themselves to this task and have learned and lived it. All the Scriptures of the world are framed to teach this one lesson; all the great teachers reiterate it. It is too simple for the world that, scorning it, stumbles along in the complex ways of selfishness.

A pure heart is the end of all religion and the beginning of divinity. To search for Righteousness is to walk the Way of Truth and Peace, and those who enter this Way will soon perceive that Immortality that is independent of birth and death and will realize that the humble effort is not lost in the Divine economy of the universe.

The divinity of a Krishna, a Gautama, or a Jesus is the crowning glory of self-denial, the end of the soul's pilgrimage in matter and mortality, and the world will not have finished its long journey until every soul has become as these and has entered into the blissful realization of its own divinity.

CHAPTER SEVEN

THE REALIZATION OF PERFECT PEACE

In the external universe, there is ceaseless turmoil, change, and unrest. At the heart of all things, there is undisturbed peace; in this deep silence, the Eternal dwells.

Human beings partake of this duality: both the surface change and unrest and the deep-seated eternal abode of Peace are contained within them.

Just like there are silent depths in the ocean that the fiercest storm cannot reach, there are also silent, holy depths in the heart of human beings that the storms of sin and sorrow can never disturb. To reach this silence and to live consciously in it is peace.

Discord is plentiful in the outward world, but unbroken harmony holds sway at the heart of the universe. The human soul, torn by discordant passion and grief, reaches blindly toward the harmony of the sinless state, and to reach this state and to live consciously in it is peace.

Hatred severs human lives, fosters persecution, and hurls nations into ruthless war, yet individuals, not understanding why, retain some measure of faith in the overshadowing of a Perfect Love. To reach this love and to live consciously in it is peace.

And this inward peace, this silence, this harmony, this Love is the Kingdom of Heaven, which is so difficult to reach because few are willing to give up themselves and to become as little children.

"Heaven's gate is very narrow and minute,
  It cannot be perceived by foolish men
  Blinded by vain illusions of the world;
  E'en the clear-sighted who discern the way,
  And seek to enter, find the portal barred,
  And hard to be unlocked. Its massive bolts
  Are pride and passion, avarice and lust."

People cry peace! peace! where there is no peace, but on the contrary, discord, unrest, and strife. Apart from that Wisdom that is inseparable from self-renunciation, there can be no real and abiding peace.

The peace that results from social comfort, passing gratification, or worldly victory does not last long and is burnt up in the heat of fiery trial. Only the Peace of Heaven endures through all trials, and only the selfless heart can know the Peace of Heaven.

Holiness alone is undying peace. Self-control leads to it, and the ever-increasing Light of Wisdom guides all pilgrims on their way. As soon as you enter the path of virtue, you partake of holiness, but it is realized in its fullness only when self disappears in the consummation of a stainless life.

Holiness alone is
undying peace.

"This is peace,
  To conquer love of self and lust of life,
  To tear deep-rooted passion from the heart
  To still the inward strife."

Reader, if you would realize the Light that never fades, the joy that never ends, and the tranquility that cannot be disturbed; if you would leave behind your sins, anxieties, and perplexities forever; if you would partake of this salvation, this supremely glorious Life, then conquer yourself. Bring every thought, every impulse, every desire into perfect obedience to the divine power resident within you. There is no other way to peace but this, and if you refuse to walk it, no amount of prayer or strict adherence to ritual, no gods or angels, will be able to help you. The white stone of the renewed life, on which is written the New and Ineffable Name, is given only to those who overcome self.

Come away, for a while, from external things, from the pleasures of the senses, from the arguments of the intellect, from the noise and the excitements of the world, and withdraw yourself into the innermost chamber of your heart, and there, free from the sacrilegious intrusion of all selfish desires, you will find a deep silence, a holy calm, a blissful peace. And if you will rest awhile in that holy place and meditate there, the faultless eye of Truth will open within you and you will see things as they really are. This holy place within you is your real and eternal self; it is the divine within you. And only when you identify yourself with it can you be said to be "clothed and in your right mind." It is the house of peace, the temple of wisdom, the dwelling-place of immortality. Apart from this inward resting-place, this Mount of Vision, there can be no true peace, no knowledge of the Divine. And if you can remain there for one minute, one hour, or one day, it is possible for you to remain there always.

> *This holy place within you*
> *is your real and eternal self;*
> *it is the divine within you.*

All your sins and sorrows, your fears and anxieties, are your own, and you can cling to them or you can give them up. You choose to cling to your unrest; you can choose to come to abiding peace. No one else can give up your sin for you; you must give it up yourself. The greatest teacher can do no more than walk the way of Truth for himself or herself and point it out to you; you must walk it for yourself. You can obtain freedom and peace only by your own efforts, by yielding up that which binds the soul and destroys peace.

The angels of divine peace and joy are always at hand; and if you do not see them, hear them, and dwell with them, it is because you shut yourself out from them and prefer the company of evil spirits within you. You are what you will yourself to be, what you wish to be, what you prefer to be. You can commence to purify yourself and by so doing can arrive at peace, or you can refuse to purify yourself and so remain with suffering.

> *You are what you will yourself to be, what you wish to be, what you prefer to be.*

Step aside, then; come out of the frenzy and the fever of life, away from the scorching heat of self, and enter the inward resting-place where the cooling airs of peace will calm, renew, and restore you.

Come out of the storms of sin and anguish. Why be troubled when the haven of peace is near?

Give up all self-seeking; give up self, and the Peace of God is yours!

Subdue the animal within you. Conquer every selfish uprising, every discordant voice. Convert the base metals of your selfish nature into the unalloyed gold of Love, and you will realize the Life of Perfect Peace. Thus subduing, thus conquering, thus converting, you will, while living in the flesh, cross the dark waters of mortality and reach that Shore upon which the storms of sorrow never beat and where sin and suffering and dark uncertainty cannot come. Standing upon that Shore, holy, compassionate, awakened, self-possessed, and glad with unending gladness, you will realize that—

"Never the Spirit was born, the Spirit will
    cease to be never;
Never was time it was not, end and
    beginning are dreams;
Birthless and deathless and changeless
    remaineth the Spirit forever;
Death hath not touched it at all, dead
    though the house of it seems."

You will then know the meaning of Sin, of
Sorrow, of Suffering and that the end thereof
is Wisdom; you will know the cause and the
purpose of existence.